Dear Judy
A new colleague who
is also a friend.
Warm

6/7/16

SEASONS

Of

THE WOLF

POETRY BY
WILLIAM ROBERT WIESNER

TO ALL THOSE WHO OPEN HEARTS TO THE MAGIC OF THIS WORLD
AND ESPECIALLY TO MY DAUGHTERS MOLLY O, AND ROBIN WHO HAVE
OPENED MINE.

TABLE OF CONTENTS

LOVE

Love

Unplanned, uncalled for

Comes of itself

Questioned

It may disappear

Like a moonbeam

When held up to the light

DAUGHTERS

If not for you

My open heart

Would close when it met

The sweet stranger who

Sits and subtly

Insinuates her self

Into my life

Cold and calculating

I would become

Concerned about

Companies and Cash flow

Caring not for what others

Cherish

A powerful person

Privileged and persevering

Pronouncing pedantic truths

I'd be pompous

And prickly

Except you two

My Sweet, Caring, Progeny

Keep me from being too much

And instead

Melt

The ice

Around my soul

And help put a welcome sign instead

PARADE

Who knows what would happen

If ripped up from here

I'm placed down somewhere new

To start a new parade

Not like my old one

I'd start it the same as the one I'm in now:

Walk down main street

Tooting my horn

And here and there

Some would join and march with me

I'd want a drummer right away

With a new easier beat

And I'd still want some cymbals

This time with a positive note

But no triangle players

We'd walk to the same beat

More or less

Picking up along the way

Trumpets, and cellos

Oboes and tubas and more

Much like now only this time with harmony

Some would be in front with me

And some would walk a bit

Then stop

Then walk some more till

At the end, when we're all together

There would be music and noise and great organized
confusion

Just before the silence

I'VE GOT A NEW GIRL

I've got a new girl

She's a lot like me

Wanting to get close

But not too close

Wanting to be near

But at a distance

Wanting to have sex

But with no mess

And she lives near-bye which means I can see her all the time

Which means Saturday night and Tuesday lunch

She's a meal in the oven

Smells good enough, but not quite ready to satisfy my hunger

Gotta tell her I want to see more of her

Gotta tell her that I want to feel more desired

Which will make her feel closed in

Which will lead to her leaving

Or mine

How do I know??

Well I've got a new girl

She's a lot like me

SPRING

This cold clammy spring

After waiting with hope for change

We talked and said

Once again that

Once again nothing had changed

And the next day's warmth

Slid

    Without penetrating

Slid

    Without cheering

Slid away

Till night's chill

Made a home for downcast

    Eyes

        Spirits

          Hopes

AIN'T NEW LOVE GRAND

When today's summer sunshine

Swept the air of soft stickiness

And made outside a joy again

I met you

No explosion but

The world disappeared

And only we were left

To do outrageous

And be outrageous

 Liberated,

We enjoyed each other's playthings

Ain't new love grand!

WORTH

Time

My friend

And enemy

As each day lived

Heads into

The past

Knowing

But not feeling

My worth

ON MY WAY TO THE GRAVE

On my way to the grave

I stopped for a while to live

Now don't get me wrong

I didn't live the whole time

      On my way to the grave

No, Sometimes I did

      What was right and useful

You know - fixing things

But when I lived , which is to say played

It was at

      Work

            Love

                        Unselfconscious self indulgence

And those times I would forget

Where I was headed

And playing in circles forget that the road I'm on is a

Dead End

WHO AM I?

The answer is clear

Though many can't see.

Who am I?

It's quite definite

I'm me!

GURU

I in amazement watch

Almost unbelieving

At how important I've become

Because of a title and some gray hairs

I'm not quite down wound from facilitating the

Registration of the twenty-two students who

All swollen with the importance of their decision

And my words

Sat themselves as attentive as

Lucky, sitting... waiting for

   His next command

Eager to obey and earn the biscuits

For which he purposes his life

DECISION TIME

Yesterday

Decision time

Mexico or not

Everyone's watching for my mistake

So I stopped

To look

Listen

Consider

And carefully think

I could hear the birds in their cages chirping

And Today when I didn't know who to call

Or even when to call

Not wanting to make a mistake I stopped

Looked

Listened

Considered

Carefully thought

Overhead, I could clearly hear the plane flying away

COLLEGE GIRL

She fell

   No

      Was propelled

Into love

So full of nice

She saw more (much more)

   Than she told

This child woman

Who stays out all night

To avoid a curfew

Then drives only where she's

Driven before

An impish seductive good-hearted

Open and secretive girl

Practicing for life

GENTLY BORN

Gently she was born

At the vicarage

By the edge of the wood

And raised well

They cultivated her

Watched her flower

Into a woman

Who

Wrote terribly wonderful

Love stories of

Violence and doom

ROSEMARY'S BIRTHDAY

Herself

  Older by a day

   Or is it a year?

Bleary eyed, hungried, restlessted

    and

Happied

    by

A day away.

SPRING SONG 1969

Spring

 And this years new love

Is still

Rosemary

SPRING SONG 1972

We hiked yesterday just the two of us

And four other people

We walked a mountain

To the top

And the mountain

Walked us down

Showing off her unfinished furniture

And creatures which she

Said weren't pets

But part of herself

Crazy mountain, but

very nice anyway,

She cushioned our steps

On her floor which

Seemed hollow

And shaded us

And showed us her Sisters

Across the valley.

SPRING SONG 1981

Time was
When
April's breeze hung
Warm and sweet

Children hopped and trotted
Crashing, clashing
Onto muddy sidewalks

And friends of summer past strolled by
To say hello and have some tea.

Time was
We were together

Now, April's breeze
Dries my
Tears

And children's joy
only echoes in some distant mind

Old friends are
Hurt and gone

I am alone
Cold and bare
Without you

There is a rainbow
Whose end you've
Reached

And the gold you
Find is dross in
My hand

While other eyes and
Smiles
Light up your day
And brighten your hard
Won treasure

I love you still, you know
And yet they say
My love with time
Will dim

Maybe so but I'm
Afraid that love doesn't
Fade
Just that-
Hearts shrink

RAIN

Wind blowing in faces

Refreshes

People leaving the water

Chilled

Leaves showing their bottoms

Dancing

The world stands still

It's going to rain.

HOMELESS

Can you hear the homeless
    Howling in the streets?
Or do you think it's just the wailing of
    Some wayward drunk
        Disturbing your reverie
           Your thoughts
                Your concentration
These bums who waste their lives
They bother me
    And I have things to do
Can you see them?
Worthless wretches
    Writhing in some
        Scummed up sewer of a gutter
Drunk or high
    On honest folks' money?
Makes me want to stay at home
Safe in Smithtown
And watch the game
    Where's the remote?

PAIN

I hold onto my pain
Like some precious stone
That anchors me
With it's weight to the center of this
Spinning world

MORE THAN MEETS THE EYE

Paused, sipping my margarita
Alive with feelings I forgot I had
    Until we met

Now like an anxious suitor
    am I
With the possibility of more

TRUE LOVE 1

Mornings
    Waiting
        For you to up and shower
While I stretch
    Thinking
        Knowing
            That
We
    Will
    Do
        Something

Wonderful
    Again
        Today
For the rest of our lives

SUMMER HEAT BLIZZARD

House bound by

This summer's heat blizzard

I look out the window

And can't believe that this is what I waited for

All winter long

SISYPHUS

I have this thought
    Not a nice one
It lurks
    Lying in wait
        Like a sapient mosquito
'til I'm feeling fine
Then,
   It wakes and bites
   Drawing just a little blood
But leaves
   An inflamed itch which
     Pulls me
       Sucks me in
         Bends my mind

Like the mirrors

In a nightmare

And then,

    Just when the welt

        Melts

           Into memory

She – my thought

Wakes

Like an old sad song

That repeats and repeats

Till it paralyzes my mind

MARTIN, MARTIN

Martin, Martin!
You gonna grow up to dah
Thas right. Die Baby Die!
You and your dreams
Ain gonna make it
Noooooo
Baby

So Fuck it man
Live it like it is
Hang your dreams.
Not your neck

You wanna do?
Wha? Wha you wanna do?
You wanna be a BIG Man --- YEAH
Well mebee so
But first--First
Martin Baby

You gonna die

Don matter how big

Or how small your dreams are

Thas all they are--dreams man --- jes dreams

Fuck em

Live it like it is

Cause Martin baby

You gonna die

Die--with those things

Those dreams

Dreams

You can't take em with you

They're wasted man--like buried money.

So listen here man

Live it like it is before ...well jes before.

PORT JEFFERSON

This morning woke me
Cool and clear
Crisp air sparkling
  my body.
The village wakes, as I
Stroll the harbor
Drinking
The deep blue water
With my eyes

THE CHOSEN

How do they do it?
Living calm and satisfied
Lives of rational passion

Sufficient unto themselves
Calm and quiet with
Screeching confidence

The day seems to bow to them
And bring them
Fortune and joy

Who are they?
I've seen so many
And never met one.

TRUE LOVE 2

Days pass
   As do years
      Like a symphony
Major movements surrounding
   A basic theme

Nuances keep it
   Exciting
      Flowing
In harmony

Atonalities too
   Distracting
      Creating tensions
         Pushing us towards the door
      Till
Harmony returns
   Softer warmer richer
      Fuller Filling

Just think
   Orange juice
   Cereal
   You
Everyday for breakfast
Forever

THINKING OF CATHY

Dawn woke me
The wind howling Cathy brushed branches
Along the rooftop

Another Cathy day to
Check the email Cathy
Shower Cathy
Breakfast Cathy

Paid some bills
Spent time on the phone Cathy
Went to the Christmas Cathy party

My walk in the neighborhood
Somehow Cathy different
Perhaps it's the newly melted snow?
Or the winter Cathy sun shining on my squinting eyes
Or maybe it's you, Cathy

BICYCLING

Into it

The steady cadence

Subtly shifting gears

To match the terrain

Back arched

Hands adjust on handlebars

The miles pass

Each like the other

Except

The curves change

And the uphills and downagains change

Pedaling in The Zone

Flowing with the scene

Sweat streaming

Heart pounding

Belonging

Stopping for a cold drink

Under the Hot Shining Sun

MAILBOX

This morning I
Once again stop
And check to see
If I am really here

Then I look out my door
down the steps
   to the foot of the driveway

Where a smoky black box
   it's red flag down

Holds (I hope) a letter for me

WASHING MACHINE

In the garage, next to the kitchen
The washing machine and dryer wait for their mission
Amongst hammers, pliers, chisels, and wrenches
Nails, nuts, cabinets, and benches

Large and white like overfed sloths
Waiting patiently for a dinner of cloth
Green kneed jeans and shirts from the garden
Towels and socks used till they hardened

All sit in a basket waiting to fill
My Maytag and Whirlpool up to the gills
Through the cycles they're soaped, bleached and softened
Sloshing and churning every so often

Comforting sounds resound in the basin
Easing my mind whenever I listen
From kerchunk of 'wash' to buzzer of clean
I love to use my washing machine

I THOUGHT OF YOU YESTERDAY

I thought of you yesterday
    And smiled
You came unsought
    In a moment of silence
        And arched my lips
And made me laugh

DAFFODILS

Diane led me to the daffodils
On a dreary, rainy day
There by her driveway, sprouted green
With swollen tips, they stood, clumped.
"Very early for daffodils," I thought

We walked this early March day
Around the lake buried in a park
On trails beaten down by horses

Here hidden away
Yet still in the suburbs
No leaves or flowers showed
The rain fell and would have chilled,
Except the rising sun of those daffodils
Warmed us

ALONE

Alone
Feels so comfortable
Like its S'posed to be

And alone feels
So bad
Like it's S'posed to be

The tightening throat
The heavy chest
The pain
Feels just about right
Like it's s'posed to be
No use fighting
There's nowhere to go
There's nothing to win
There's no one to beat

Just me

REMEMBER TO FORGET

Sometimes late at night
When I forget that I forgot you
I can taste you
And your musk
Fills me
Smokes me like leaves from an
Autumn fire
And then
Forgetting I forgot
I remember
Orange ice and sitting by the summer stream
smiling and hugging
Making love and loving you
You beautiful
In your dress and bare bottom
Losing the car keys
Playing the recorder
Boggle and the Times

Musing

Forgetting

Will you hold me?

And stand by me?

And love me?

And share me, and share you?

And… and…

And then I remember

I remember to

Forget

And recollect that

We don't speak,

Or touch

Or think

Of each other

Anymore

SLIPPING INTO THE SHADOWS

I am going to slip into the shadows
Not the stuff Legends are made of

Still a man who has made
A mark
A legacy
Only the signature, in my case,
Will erode with time

Damn it!!
I want them to know
It was me
Me who thought and plotted
And built against
Strong odds
The... the.... The....

I know I built something but...
I can't think of what

HORSES AND DOGS

Horses and dogs
    Running in the field
Up the hill
    Claiming the earth
Proud owners
    Omnipotent heroes
They chase the
    Wolves and lions away
Stomping the brush
They snort and bark their power
The sun and clouds
    Race away from their thundering feet
Hiding behind the skirts of night
Lest they be torn from the heavens
Howling at the moon
    Sleeping while standing
Lords of the world
Their minds then do quiet
While they stare
Their big eyed wild animal inscrutable stare
And sniff
The fence

CALM BEFORE THE STORM

She seems the calm before the storm
    Or is it the eye?

Hard to tell on First Impressions
But the storm is there
    Swirling, intense—
        Listen close
Closer and you can hear the wind waiting, working
    The surf up against the shore
For now the dike holds and the
    Unwrinkled surf is as calm as
The soft breeze of a summer's day

HELL'S PHOENIX

Bang Big, Big Bang
Birthing pain of Cosmos
Not swan of Leda
Or Mary's dove
But Hell's phoenix

LOST

Let me out
I want to be
    Free
Let me out
I want to be
    Me
So lost
    Lost
        Lost
I invent that
I'm found

DYING

I've come into my manhood only, just in time to die

Or is dying what brings me to manhood

Freed from the "shoulds" and "oughtas"

Since there no longer is a penalty for being me

Writing out of me instead of

    The grammar book, and painting

The pictures that lie within that

Don't look, can't look like this world since my world isn't

this world it's

mine and now I'm tired of making my world look like this

or … your

world

Here in my youth, at 50

Actually my old, old age; I can be bad

Write obscenities afraid of nothing

Since nothing is

All that beckons

I regret, I do regret

But now in my manhood

In my few minutes of manhood

I also live

STICKY

Yawning

Up from slumber

You squeeze my arm

As I lumber

Off the bed

Into the bath

To wash away the sticky memento

Of last night's excesses

WINTER

When that winter came
And froze my soul
And left no room for warmth

You came and sang
Your song

Somehow you grew a garden
There,
In that winter

O MISTRESS MINE

O mistress mine
Your neck divine
I dare to kiss
And stir some bliss

Your lips do tempt
And stir my need
To stroke your breast
And more, indeed

My pride does swell
At words so warm
I long to quell
Your shaking storm

By penetrating touch
And soothing sips
By gentle touch
'pon swollen lips

I'm yours my dear
To take in hand
Or blow away
Atop the sand

Or better yet
To take me in
Deep in that space
Where all begins

CYBERLOVE

It's been cold this spring
    Especially at night when
        The sun sets and the wind comes up
The thermostat doesn't know it and
    Leaves the furnace to rest unlit and still
While I sweater up and put a cap
    On my head to keep me warm
Until…
Until I met you…
The cool electron version
    That lights up my screen
Or sets the phone to vibrating
The gentle smile and warm
    Mellifluous voice
Penetrates the cold shell
I take off my hat
    My sweater
        My…. Everything
And burn
    HOT
        For you

FRUSTRATION

Our sweet soft kiss brings back
The years of hand-holding friendship
Memories of music, laughter, and arguments settled
The desire of the years folded into a moment of time

That kiss, the kiss you love
Is, for you, the dessert
For me the kiss I love
Is the appetizer that quickens
My appetite, my desire, my deepest longings

Which now,

Have no place to go

SEPARATION

Sweetly, silently she
Passes
From this life
To that

A few ripples mark
Her way
Her smile
Remains

Like a dagger

CLOUDS

Clouds
Bulky as mountains
Crying themselves
into
Nothingness

GREEN DEATH

Death
Warm and green
Fertile goddess
Smiling Queen

Giver of life

THE WALLS ARE HIGH

The walls are high
They always are when
I get near enough to
Climb them

They scare me not
The walls so high but
Them that see me
Scaling
Their eyes do judge and
Find me weak, unfit to
Be and
Failing

I want to be
Back in the arms of
One who'll soothe
And keep me warm

She can not be
This one I need
Save in the end by
Dying

Till then I try
To prove I can when
Tis true I can't
It's shaming

And shamed I am
From dawn to dawn
A man not sure
Of being

Where is the lie
That I'll believe
So I'll forget
My yearnings

I'm doomed to fail
Although successed
By those that judge
Around me

The walls are high
They always are when
I get near enough to
Climb them

They scare me not
The walls so high but
Them that see me
Scaling

HIPPY

I saw a hippy with braces today
On his teeth
Yeah!
He had long dark hair
Curly-but not too
Touched his shoulders-you know
And very pretty

AND THE CLOCK TICKED

And the Clock ticked
And ticked
Long into the night
Eerily stealing the silence
Taking it out of earshot

ALL THESE INSIGHTS

All these insights
Deep to the pulp
    Truths
That find their way to the surface
Now that I'm
Distracted

See some good comes
Even in the worst of times
Even these worst of times
When waking is too much to bear

My mind has expanded
I understand, better
    My drives and what drives me
So much more complete than before
Even while feeling empty

But this rational bullshit is no good
All that is real
    Is the pain
This thrum thrum dull toothache
Pain in my soul
This sharp ripping pain in
My heart

Nothing else is real
All those truths read
Like some out of date novel
Warming like a fireflies light

TOMORROW

I seem to be addicted to tomorrow
What is already, is old
Not scintillating, exciting, sexy

Today doesn't answer why or even why not
Talking to the same old people
About the same old same old

Now is:
    Full of ideals and empty of hope
    Full of love and devoid of affection
Full of spiritualness and alone in the universe

Tomorrow:
    I meet the girl of my dreams and live in an
    unending romantic haze
    I meet and speak with God who, in a non-
    patronizing tone rxplains and shows me the
    clockworks of the Universe and why we really need
    a universe anyway
    I find peace in that central secure place and am
    always excited by life
    Death becomes an understood friend
Tomorrow is the lynchpin which brings
    Excitement
    Answers
    And order to the tiresome chaos of
Today

So….
Goodnight and Good Morning!!!!

THE SINGLE GIRL

I think they hate me   Damn them
 And I think they fear me   The bastards
Jollying up and cozying up
Making me believe it's me making
  Them Jolly and Cozy
Smiling and sweetly talking
  Caressing with words to
Win my good wishes that I might favor them with
A held hand, a kiss with parted lips
A warm soft breast to suck up to
Oh, And I give them that,
  And that and more
I hold and stroke and
I too sweetly talk and
  Meekly (at first) fondle
Happy to touch and together
Share
All because they want me
  And treat me well
    And seem to love me
But after they've touched and talked
  And (not so) gently gentled me
Filled me and brought me out
Slowed time, slowed the world
  Enough so it can be touched and tasted
Led me to believe that there is time to sit and savor
I hear their steps,
  See them move
Away
  Running......
    From me??? From themselves?

Leaving me alone to clean their cum

TOWARDS YOU

Waiting for the rain to stop
    Wind to ease
        Conversation to cease

Waiting
    To begin work
        So it can end and

I'm free to
    Put the key in the ignition
        And get on the road

Towards You

NEW LOVE

You Got Me
I was there, confident, cool, smiling
And yes, a little depressed
Without a partner for so long
Not alone
But not sharing
And you got me,
And I got you
Conversation so easy
Sex and banter
Puzzles and dinners
Not threatened by former attachment
Supportive of family and relationships
Honest (to a fault?)
Like a couple married for years
Comfortable
Safe
Loving
Without enough excitement
I loved it all.

JAMESVILLE RESERVOIR

"Get out of the water!"
"Stop crying"
"Johnny where are you?"

A kid dunked up and down
    by his brother
Another dragged in
    against his will
Another "Mommy, Mommy
    watch me dive!"

Getting splashed- and wincing
    Before you plunge in yourself
Then jumping in all at once
("This is the last time, Get out of the water")
Smiles on kids jumping up and down in the water
Splashing
  each other
   and me

Shivering kids, refusing
  to admit they're cold
Yelling
  Screaming
Immersed
  A thousand kids
   In one liquid body
Laughing
Shrieking
Shivering
Smiling
Look at me-ing kids

and parents burning in the sand
Watching
Vicariously enjoying the 1000 headed body

   and teenagers
        showing themselves off
   showroom style
      (look but don't touch)

Frisbying
Mothers changing their children
Fathers forcing them in the water
Waiting half an hour for
   an overpriced bottle of pop
        (warm)

Playing cards, drinking beer
Fishing
Picnicking
Ordered out of the water

Swimming on sea weeds
Too hot-into the water-nice
   Too cold-out of the water-nice
      Too hot

Barefoot stepping onto
Grass
Rocks
   and
Caterpillars

Sitting in the sun
Getting knocked out, doing
Nothing

FLYING TO YOU

I came across the sky
In one of those silver Eagles
Me... In the belly of the beast

Across vast plains of white clouds
going to the horizon
Over ancient sculpted mountains their
Naked hoary heads covered in snow

Past maybe a million people
Lost in the reality of their lives

Roaring as we came
Hungry,
Reaching for the other side of
This land
Down to the bay
And you

DEATH

Pained and Poisoned
By life you
Have kept faith
By faith
And were found unwanting

God in loveless limbo
Is warmed
By your gentle presence

Soon,
Too soon
You and he will
Mutually embrace.

TIMING

It was a rough winter that left

The fields frozen

And the landscape barren

Of produce

Green there was and

Plenty of young shoots

But buds were bit by cold

All hope

Gone with that

Unexpected frost

A week later

Or two

And buds secure

In strength would

Have held in them

Next years seed

Now, nothing is left but last years hope

The present though green is

Pale and Bitter.

And then I stumble
Upon a bit of
meadow protected
From wind and frost
Oh wise mother how then
Was born such a
Stupid son
To pick a fruit
Before its time
And imagine it
Sweet.
Impatient fool
To kill with
Greedy hope
What still survives
Wiser than I
The fecund fruit
Whose stem held
Firm against my pull
Perhaps it will survive to ripen in
Its good time,
And undamaged, grow

SHORT STUFF

Locally Gusty
   Bedeviled Bob
Enlightened hears
Terpsichorally
Like snow falling off a roof
Slowly imperceptibly grumble
   Growling
SPLAT

Busy
Extorted world
Doing what its told
At the point of a watch

Rumble train
Clack along the dull rails
To stop at dingys
Called stations

BAD LITTLE BOY

Remember when
    You
       Were young
And running late for school
Everybody saw
    You
And knew what a
  Bad little boy
    you
       were

FIREFLIES

Fireflies. their night's hunt

Brings no trophy

Their blinking only

A passing

Pleasure

And the next night

They send the same

Signal once again

Moving results in

No movement

Lighting

Produces no heat

Their visible forms

Mask their lack of substance

Fly away and

Look some more

You sorry souls

And when you despair

Of finding your way

Then…..

REDHEAD

Sitting at the soda fountain

Strawberry soda served up

Red and frothy

Sharp

    And Wet

           And Satisfying

Not too sweet

With seeds caught between teeth

I'd like another please

HOT HALLOWED GROUND

This hot hallowed ground

That tests my soul

Lures me till, I'm lost

Work and play distract me from being

Bringing me to a jagged edge

To be forged in the hot hell

Fires of every day living

I walk thirsting

Trying this and that and that again

Burning with desire

Distracted from rest

Until

I'm with you

Your cool spring water

And shading trees

Bid me to sit down and rest

And be me

You…my oasis of riches

In this desert

E-MAIL DATE

Tomorrow
> Tomorrow the word
>> The word is made flesh

After – yes after the
> Tsunamis of passion passes-
>> Crashes

We will be left-
> Still
>> Peaceful
> Still
>> Together
> Still
>> Full

Of each other or....
>> Bereft

Still...
> After the phantasmagorical fantasy
>> The alluring illusion
>>> The private passion

Reality...
> Is welcome

TEASE

This dance
This stormy dance of
Saying goodbye
Two steps forward, two to the right
And one backwards

Conversation that swirls and twirls around
What can't be said
Flavored conversation, empty
As the unfelt breeze that
Flutters the leaves at twigs end
Till
They fall

This modern dance,
This no touch pirouette
This inner rhythm rite of passage, which
Like the wind
Moves us

GONE

Gone, the waves from pounded beaches
Wind from polished peaks
Grass and trees from scented earth
Buildings from the streets

The time to see and hear is past
To feel and taste the sun
To pain and sweat and laugh and yearn
To wallow in the earth

Why did we try to live at all
To breathe and fight and war
Why did we work and strive and play
When life itself is death

PILLSBURY

This bread is stale though
    Freshly baked from Pillsbury
    Dough Boy's flour bought
    At the local A & P
    The recipe's from the N.Y. Times Cookbook
    Bought at Waldenbook's
    After eating at Friendly's
    Or was it McDonald's

    I can't figure
        Why this new bread
            Tastes old

    I'll eat something else
    While shopping at the mall
    First Macy*s and Florsheim's followed by
    K and B toys or maybe Toys R Us
    Sears for tools and some pillows

Sometimes I don't know if it matters where I live
America you've become one expansive
And mediocre town where living in
Tucson or Syracuse differs only in
Temperature and unseen vistas

I want to go home!
But it's everywhere

VERMONT

Gentle mountains rolling, rising
Forcing clouds to climb their peaks
Before they fall to fill the valley
Inch by wooly inch till
We are in that warm wet blanket.

The birds sing here, The air breathes free
And easy up the chimney the wood
Fire's smoke spices the land.
Mornings up from summer's sleep
The silent scene gives rest
Cow's low, Horses trot
The tractors whine and saws
Cut the day in pieces.
I can still see the green hills
That stood so firm and
Stayed my heart
And gave breath
To my soul

SUBURBIA

This inbetween place
This comfort zone
Of air, music, trees
And close cropped lawns
We made it in our 1 families
Kept the niggers
    Oh excuse me, Blacks out too
Except the white ones

We read Thoreau
    And Keats
        And Paine
Our children take piano

But we never fuck
    Or excite
        Or are afraid
            Or demand
And worst
We never get lost

FORMAL DINNER (COOPERSTOWN)

We all said hello
And smiled
With self satisfied
Feelings of purpose

And gathered in a heap
To our tables of
  Bland Beef and
    Fellow workers

Then awaited the
  Honored guest's
Talk of responsibility to man

We clapped and left
Nobody said Goodbye.

AWARDS CEREMONY (COOPERSTOWN)

Jack sat and watched
   And Listened
      Focused on the Flautist

      While

Frank slept and fidgeted and
   Fred studied his speech

The Audience watching it's collective watch
Grew restless
As Tilden and Johanna stared out

Too long they thought
   Too long
      They all thought
Except Jack
   Who sat and watched
And Listened
   Focused on the Flautist

LIZARDS

Lizards our long lost parents
Living on as echoes in our mind
Lizards no cure or enchantment
For these immortal teamster
Masters of our thoughts
I dream of them huge and hungry
Clutching the neck and shoulders
Of children
Grown into men
They whisper
Always
Quietly bending
Slowly turning
Our will to theirs
They shout
Nonsense noises
Confusing, discordant, screeching
Sounds that
Mask, distort
The inner voice
That clear bell inner voice...that voice which could,
Like light, point the way
Lizards
    Scaly things
Once warm
Walking among the hooves
Of untamed wild things
Stampeding, frightened
Pitiful things
Longing for the safety of
A harness

YOU IN THIS LOVELESS LANDSCAPE

I'd rather be with you then
Alone
   In this loveless landscape

Because you, when you're sweet
   Massage my soul to sanity
And you, when you're kind
   Raise flowers and make tea

And you keep me busy figuring you out
   Which is better than
Feeling alone in this loveless landscape

PLUGGED IN

Plugged in to you
    I'm connected
    Me the all powerful
        Versatile
        Amusing
    Appliance
    Still needs a source of energy

    With my rocket in
        Your socket
    Which is close to the main grid- I am
    Unlimited
    But then who are you?
    Source of power, or vehicle?
    Person or connection?
    Strong assertive or weak passive?
    What matter…
    You my energy
    Me your function

WALKING AWAY

I keep trying to move away
By walking backwards
So I can look for your secret smile
And laughing eyes

I not only bump into things
I don't get very far

Perhaps I should do a 180
Then you
Won't obscure my horizon

But when I try it's always
A full 360

Dearie Me!

SNEAKERS

Gooshin mud in sneakers is fun

Not bare toed fun

But its only spring the first

And still cold

And I'm not a kid anymore

TIME AND AGAIN

Time and again

  we meet and

Time and again

  we meet again

THE TRAIN

When the train comes by
The long one that starts back when
And ends down the road apiece

And stops – it always stops twice –
Once to pick up a few new souls
And again – to drop off a few older ones

They usually know when to get on, and where
But almost always forget their last stop
Until they discover that the train
Has left them by

The older ones understand
But when a young one forgets
And gets off
And the train leaves
Hell, that's when I want to get off too

NO TO LOVE

Had I been able to say

No Love

    Then

I might not be saying

No to love

Now

Had I put you first

With love

    Then

Remembering to love me first

I might have your love

Now

Had I not been afraid

To risk us

    Then

I might not have

Lost us

Now

Because you Love

Were so good

    Then

That I could not hurt with small no's

Until, I must hurt with a big NO to us

Now

But thanks

    For being good

        And honest

           And caring

               And there

    Then

And for being (mostly) strong

Now

It's true

I loved you

    Then

And care for you

    Still

But it's also true that

You and I are not Us

Anymore

JOHN LENNON

I, Idly stand by

While autumns wind

Leaves leafless feathery

Branches to tickle the sky

And John Lennon died last night.

We

   All of us

Die too young

FIRST DATE

I hardly know you
But you're gone
And I feel empty

The scent you wore
Lingers on my lips
And I know my face will
  Remain unwashed

You're like a cherub
Laughing and singing
In tune with life

You're to be wanted
 and cherished
But never had

I Love You now!

SUNNY SKIES

Sunny skies on
   Warm days
Shining on people
   Confined by darkness

WORRY BEADS

Worry, Worry little beads
You can't be rubbed wrong
   (or right)
Filling up with master's energy
Becoming bigger
   More important with
Each mantra that sings
   Over you

Power to heal

OUT OF SORTS

At times like these when
   out of sorts
Searching for who knows what
I fret a lot
My stomach churns and my
Bowels empty their poisons
Continuously

My tongue yearns to do the same
Blasting him, her, the world to
Bring them down to
Common filth
That I walk, swim in.

THE DOG

Where does the dog lie
That barked
And chased the
Bike away?

Clean white dog
Brown spots and a
Black patch over
A wrinkled, reddened eye

Running and laughing
Spittle-ing
Immersed in its
Own boundless power
Sprung from its chain
Through the hole in the fence
After the flickering
Spokes of the silver
Schwinn

Down the safe silent
Street
Through the confusing
Catacombed corridors
Of suburban houses

To the lazy laned
Avenues where
A red Buick taught
Some manners
To our wayward hound
And chased him
Crying through yards
And gardens where ·
Now he lies,
Lost or worse

JANE

I look at the world through Jane colored glasses

Her face figures in every view

No steel grey sedan

Rolls by that she doesn't sit in

No straight shoulder length

Strawberry blond is not her

Every conversation has her Laugh

Or comment, or pout

Or sigh

I hunger for her,

Like I hunger to eat chocolate

Placed in my hand

I long to see

And savor and taste her,

And yes, I want to love her'

But she has slipped away

No longer here except

As a lens distracting my view

How I long to take these Jane Colored glasses off

And

    Live

GRAND SCHEMES

Grand schemes and plans
Of fame and fortune
Pass, with time, away
From me, and leave

An empty, pallid, view
Of unearthly earth

WITCHES

Witches with
Wide seductive
Lustful smiles
Sweet lips
Camouflaging fetid breath
And rank mouth

Filthy with power
Moving broomsticks
Through the air
   Disembodied
   Enlarged, disfigured
Wands
Changed as she changes
From Fairy to Witch

Insatiable this Bitch
Demanding, expecting
 Complete fealty
Her Unfillable, insatiable cunt
Requiring full-fill-ment
Eating and spitting out
The bones of the boys
Who feed her

Whence comes this power?
Given freely by those who
Wish to taste freedom

This siren's song
Is the heart of bondage

Cut these bonds
Survive the witch
Fuck her till she
Spills over sated with
Semen saying…. No More

Only then
Can the darkened cave
Be left behind
The boy leave a man
Freedom is walking away
Full of seed
Caring not for her blood lust
　　Or her magic
　　　　　Or her finger on your
Heart and in your soul

Be careful
Killing her strengthens her
Fucking her creates her desire
Caressing her makes her ugly and harsh
Harshness makes her pretty and vulnerable
She has everything
And gives nothing
Victory is essential
And seems impossible
For her hole never fills, and her lust never abates
Can our yearning ever cease?

TIME PASSES

Time passes
The face that etched my heart
Slowly fades away
Leaving a shadow soul
To warm my days
And chill my nights

MY GOAL

My goal
To be successful in life
To pound the drum of victory
And blow the trumpet of success
To look back and be proud
Of deeds, and non-deeds
With medals, and degrees
And luncheons to remember
To make my life worthwhile
For it to have reason
 But I
Like you my friend
Will find all drums hollow
And trumpets make the noise of hot air
The medals are tin and cheap
The degrees forgotten
The luncheons turned to waste
There is no reason except
The reality

SAFE HARBOR

Times are when
I've enough had
And wishing to be through
Dream away (far) of others

Varied smells
Colors, contours
And crevices
Draw me - bend my mind
Away

Hassles and haggling
Tired and worn
Haggard I seek
Refreshment

When I look away
Sensual fantasies
But when I look deeper
There's nothing

And then I see you-really
With newly cleared eye and
Burnished heart
Closer we get
and closer still
Till
We still ourselves
Entwined And it's wonderful.
Easy steady glow
of contentment and bliss
Smooth flowing from Solid center
We belong to each other Mind, body and soul

For you, my love
Anchor me in safe harbor,
Freeing me to roam
This turbulent void
When   ever I will

AUTUMN

Autumn
   A new season's coat
Of golden scales warms
The ground and cheers the eye

SONG OF LIFE

The song of life is a chorus of voices
A rhythm of action cacophony of sound
Somewhere in space a voice
     Sang
Out In the wilderness, and echoed on itself to
     Create
New vibrations and subtleties which echoed to
     Repeat
What had already happened in new ways
     Until
The source got lost and the myriad voices
     Forgot
That they were reflections of the single
     Whisper

NAKED TRUTH

She slipped her day's persona on

Foundation garments of ambition and smarts

A sheer top that exposed yet softened

A tailored suit that reflected power and efficiency

At the end of the day

    She sometimes forgot to disrobe

And would carry all that weight with her through the

night into the next day

But when she did

And she stood bare naked

Her faults showed

And her insecurities

And the gray roots

And the fear of being wrong

And the fear of Just Being

Afraid yet hopeful

Only then was she finally beautiful

Only then was she finally herself

RED STALLION

I curse them
These wounded boys
Who want and hate
    Who need and fear
    Who come and run

I need them too
To touch my cheek
And brush my thigh
And part my aching, waiting, wet lips

I want them to ride that fierce
    Red Stallion
Into the bottomless pit
Shouting, Screaming, plunging into
Forever

NIGHT

Night thought to gain a bit
Perhaps by sneaking up on Day
When Day wasn't looking
She thought to steal some time
And so she hid
Behind a boulder shaped
    Mountain high, Grey cloud
She woke early
Put on her downy slippers
    So her dark cushioned presence
        Was even softer than usual
And slipped undercover
    Into the cloud
Turning it into a
Black, deep, dark, brooding thing
Like a puma ready to spring

Thus hidden she scudded toward the afternoon sun
And then
just as Success was sure
Day turned and poured some Rays of pure white
    Into that soggy collection of smoke

No room for Night
Her angry retreat
Boomed
    Across the land
The trapped light now escaped
    Earthward
And her angry tears
Hailed
Day's victory

THE CITY

Did you go into the city
Taste the ice cream
And smell the urine
Soaked streets?

Did you go into the city
Cross the bridge
See the lights
And feel the fine thrum,
Thrum, thrum,in the air?

Did you go
And walk the streets
Shop the stores
And eat
    Someplace special
        And weird?

And did you see a show
And spot a pimp or street walker
    In gaudy dress
    Outside an XXX movie??

Did you feel more alive
    More real
        More at home
            And more excited?

Or less?

PORT JEFFERSON II

I thought of you today
When summer's sun had
Slowly set
Leaving a bright
Orange glow
To paint the
Water
And silhouette
The ships in the harbor

FRIEND

How nice
To see you
After all this time
And find you're still a friend

I knew you right away, you know
By the way you hold your self
Surprised?
Did you think I wouldn't recognize you
When I've always loved you?

We talked
Emptily in many ways, but
The real messages weren't verbal
They were deeper
And understood by My Self

How nice to see you

CUTTING THE CORD

Yesterday I
    Tossed your plate out
The one you brought
    From Israel
A throwaway from the start
It dropped and broke on its way

Today I
    Drank from your mug
The white one with
Red ladybugs
That sat dry
And unused for
Four full months

Yesterday I
    Found the cord
That bound me to you
Today
    I cut it

THE SUBURBS

I used to sneer at them

Washing their cars

Mowing their close cropped lawns

Fertilizing

How they wasted precious time

Time they could have spend

    Reading or writing or

        Seeing a play

Me? I thought a lot

    Worried a bit

Wrote some

And was very productive

Now I've joined that army

I wash my car

    Sow, rake

        And mulch

Plant my seed

Fertilize

I love to play outside

7-11

The kids outside still scare me
Like they have for 30 years
Milling about
    Talking
    And smoking
Hair a statement
High energy exploding

Insults and stares
Reaching towards some
Target

Me?
I pray
For invisibility

HALLOWEEN

A time for masks on masks
Costumes on costumes
The false more real
Than the true

Come walk naked-
Put on a mask

SYRACUSE RALLY AFTER KENT STATE

Singing their songs
   Joyous dirges
And heard the speeches
   Epithet
      Epitaphs
The young demanding
   Freedom and life
      Cheered
The death of guardsmen
And decided to freak out
In order to gain support
They gathered for freedom
   And tried
      To trample her flag

They were right
   But God
      They were wrong

SHADOW SOUL

The shadow soul so swift and fleet

That moves, eludes our searching feet

That lies entire with music's beat

Responds to all

Time isn't

CAR'S RUMBLING

Cars

Rumbling groaning

  Watched carefully

    for mistakes

Exercises the eyes

  Stiffens the neck

    Wearies shoulders

For a day of

Resting, relaxing, sunning

  Shoulder standing, non-productiveness

CONFLICT?

Who are you Christian?

Proud possessor of the God who dies

We know the Christ

Inside he dwells and pleads our case

With the spirit

Who are you Hebrew?

That you spurn salvation

Rejecting the love of God?

Cannot you see you are

Chosen to suffer

Repent and believe in the Son

Your fascination, Why?

Because we spurn Christ?

Is your faith shaken

Or are you become us?

The Wanderer

Soul separate Soma

We are the example

Wisdom binds the two

We are all saved

STARCH

Starch granules
With laminations
To shield against
Perturbations
　In
　　The
　　　Amount
　　　　Of
　　　　Sun

LONELY

My Friends are lonely too
　All the time,
Within the walls of their well warmed homes
Curtained walls with pictures and attached lamps
Walls, painted and marked
By friends and children
Which become the boundaries
Beyond which the world
Is cold and barren of feelings
But also
The boundaries
Within which restless souls search for comfort by
Listening to the stereo
Turning on the TV
Preparing pop corn
Reading
Writing
Ranting on the phone
Looking for something to do
And someone to love

A FLOWER

A flower grows this side of the shore

One that I've seen, felt and

Detected the odor of

A flower grows..the old one is there no more

This one is new to me

Suspended

Waiting in mid-air

For the slightest puff of wind to send me

Moving, rushing, hurricaning

Towards some destiny I don't even glimpse

Somehow what once was

Isn't

Time is used to deaden the pain

But it prolongs the agony

Let's be done with it now… not tomorrow

I don't love you less for knowing this

But I won't love you more for not letting me go

I don't want to leave you

Please send me away

BIGGER HILL

If it were possible yo climb this hill
I think I would
  Just to see, as
I've been told-
  The bigger one
That lies beyond

DEEP DOWN INSIDE

Deep Down inside
I look for that little seed
That kernel of
Shadowed light
   Waiting to bloom
Alas that seed lies
Dormant
Entombed by
   Doubt, guilt, fear
As it sits
Moldering in the dank dark crevices
Of my soul

FUTURE PATH

The future path I tread upon
Looks empty to me now
I would that I could change my view
But the question here is how?

I see the end of all good things
Of fish and plants and men
I see the God I had at birth
Torn loose from his heaven

My child grows and takes delight
In friends and dogs and play
I cry at night to think of when
She'll see the world turned gray

And all the evil works of man
Shall turn upon him then
The world will end in poisoned war
The stars will shine again

LIVING SAFE

Is it better to live in the shadow
of some dark sleepy mountain
Safe from rain
    And the raging north wind
Than to climb the treacherous slopes
And feel the warmth of the sun

Is it better to live in dark musty pools
Safe from pounding surf
    And the hurricanes furious roar
Than to swim some swift stream
And see the children at play

Is it better to live in airless buildings
Tenured and safe from poverty's stench
Than to range with your mind
And see the world dancing

COOPERSTOWN

Raining, we left
In darkness
Cars slowly moved
Blocking our way

Trees in October
Dressed in green
All the way to Kingston
Drab (How can green be drab)
With sad promises
Of next week's loss of color

PAUL

Dear Paul,
I'd love to write a poem
   Of you, for you
But I can't
I'd like to capture you in a few simple words
But it won't be done

Perhaps a picture in words
But where are the boundaries?
A description of your abilities, your successes?
But words for a painter, musician, craftsman, ...?

No, it can't be done
I won't do it
But I am so glad to know you
To hear and see you
To feel your presence
To be your friend

HUGE POTENTIAL

Huge potential
Chemistry that took off

And Grew

Ahhh the Exploration

Mind and Body

Emotions

Commonality and
not so commonality

A few weeks later

Love And

Getting familiar
.....until

A small fight

    Little annoyance

        Unanswered phone

Still Love

    But growing frustration

        Less passion

Working thru a tough weekend

    Resentment

        Annoyance

Love is still declared

    But someone else shows up

        With chemistry

Still Talking

    Some Jokes

        But nothing's left

SNOW

Slick city gearing up for days work
Bustle, cars move, people weave in and out
Crowds, factories start, smoke air
Talk, trade deal
Buy   mountains
Sell   lakes
Noise, clatter, cars, boom, boom,
  Gnarl, Crash, talk , deal
The weather teller   low pressure
Snow squal   s l o w   s t e a d y
Slow white wafers wile their way
Meet fellows softly settle
     No sound,
Less - absorbing sound
Painting the valley with white
drifting soft curves, graceful peaks
Growing slowly, gently taller
Then wind, from where?
  Driving down, whipping flakes into fury
  Drowning the city in softness
Cars stop, powers out, stores close,
People hold warmth
The gentle earth our always mother
Mocks our power laughs at our delusions
Teaches humility where we're willing to learn
Inside we understand
Carless streets drive smiles to our faces
Hellos to our mouths, pleasure to our senses
There is a way,
  We can bend with the wind
  Move with the snow
  Dance with the earth

DISTANCE

The jarring jokes I tell
    The puns and slapstick humor
Some laugh out loud
    Others smile
But I stare ahead

The clever anecdotes
    Tales of travel and intrigue
Some lean forward
    Other nod their heads
I watch their eyes

The strong shoulder
    Understanding voice
She cries and talks
    And pours out her heart
I listen from afar

MR. GARDNER

Mr. Gardner
Planting seeds
Of knowledge
By force

Mrs. Gardner
Waters Mr. Gardner
    And
Grown his acorns

FLAME

Flame
    Burning my soul

Wilderness Bush
    Remaining unquenched by

Holy Water or
    Bread, not risen

WOODS OF DESPAIR

Walking the woods of despair
In half-lit skies
Of gray and blue
We turn with hope
And look

      and

Turn once more

THE FARMER

Gardens of Greening Beans
    Stand in moist dirt
Sweating their juices and
      Working harder n hell
    While waiting for
The coverall'd man
With the wrinkled eyes

COWS

Big brown cow eyes
Staring in terror wildly at and away
from me

Trapped by the head that's locked into
Vertical poles of
Eat and get fat and
Give milk

Suffer your fate that we
Might drink your unspent life

LOSS

I saw you yesterday and
    Since then
I haven't seen any flowers
    Or heard the birds

Music that used to thrill
    Grates against the
        Conversations in my head

And the lump in my chest is
    Filled with pain
        Too Big
            For Screams

FREEDOM

Flowers open as
The sun conducts
And leaves dance as the
Wind instructs
My dog
Comes to my call
While the cat
Plays with the ball
The game is played
With rules set out
And each takes his turn
To do what's about
No questions are asked
For queen nature
Dictates the movement
As reactions mature

I see the teacher
Doing his thing
Driven to instruct
Satisfying his being
And the soldier too
Out to fight
No questions asked
Just do or die
So where am I?

What's my base?
What do I play?
Do I have a place?
Out of step
To an unheard drum
Looking and waiting
For my time to come
I was born
But am I free
With full discretion
Of what to be?
Can I choose my game
And pick my place
From a universe???
How?? There's too much space
Curse my freedom
Take it away
Tell me what to do
Tell me which game to play
Read my cards!!
Look at the stars!
I Ching or crystal ball
Take me from this choice of horrors
Damn it all
Damn free will
I want to be told
How else to fulfill?

Tell me, tell me
Someone!! Where am I, What's wrong?
Move me someplace
I want to belong

NO ROOM

I've got no best friend room left

I'm fullup with buddies

    Pals, loves, and lovers

Some still are and

    Some are, still

Alive, present or gone

They've left no room

For you

HEART OF HEARTS

If people knew what went on
    In my heart of hearts
Probed the empty depths
    Looking for the substance
How disappointed they would be

The shifting currents bent
    By your opinion and theirs
A foundation of loose blocks
    With more added
        Shakily
            Each year
A Tower
    Always ready to collapse
No wonder I'm afraid
No wonder my door is closed
No wonder I don't invite you in
    To sit side by my side in front of the fire.

LEAN DOWN

Lean down God
I need you
And standing is hard

What is going on here?
There's pushing and grabbing
And God…there is fear

Why is it all?
The countless circles
The endless hall

Is the end the end?
Is nothing gained?
Please God…Help Me
Comprehend

DEED ME NO DEEDS

Deed me no deeds
And will me no wills
Let me go out and
Dwell in the hills

Alone

I would walk
Trite and naked
To find what's been found
And live untutored
To rediscover again
What has not been lost

COFFEE BREAK

Coffee now,
To while away a minute
Or ten

Escape
To a caffeine sea
With sugar sand

To steel the soul
For another attack of
Work

BAXTER

He was already old when I met him

Lots of gray among the black hairs,

He got up slowly

And walked carefully

Till he got outside

Outside he was young

Walking slow and careful until

We crossed into the park

And Then,

Then the transformation

In a moment he was lit up

Like a firecracker

Bounding

Running

Jumping a fence and

Exploring with puppy like

Enthusiasm

He passed,

We all pass

And we miss him

POETRY

Flowing along
The Poem
   Pours
      Itself
         Downhill
Stops to think---

And   falls
  apart

I AM THE WOLF

I am the wolf

So long buried in sheep's clothing
That now I smell of sheep
   talk like a sheep
Eat and sleep like a sheep
Almost forgetting that
I am the wolf
So Beware
Under, yes under the cloak I lie in wait
Pretending sleep,

But,
I am the wolf
Smart, strong
Predatory

I hunt
Food, favors, sex
On my terms

Innocent as a sheep

Dumb as a sheep

Weak as a sheep

You want to give to me

Give to the innocent

Give to the dumb

Give to the weak

Give to …….. me

But

I am the wolf

Beware

Don't let me loose

Don't unleash my anger

Don't threaten my loves

Don't challenge me

Don't make me remember

To take off the sheep's clothing